Our Bodies

Our Hearts

Charlotte Guillain

Heinemann LIBRARY

www.heinemannlibrary.co.uk
Visit our website to find out more information about Heinemann Library books.

To order:

☎ Phone +44 (0) 1865 888066
🖨 Fax +44 (0) 1865 314091
💻 Visit www.heinemannlibrary.co.uk

Heinemann Library is an imprint of Capstone Global Library Limited, a company incorporated in England and Wales having its registered office at 7 Pilgrim Street, London, EC4V 6LB – Registered company number: 6695582

Heinemann is a registered trademark of Pearson Education Limited, under licence to Capstone Global Library Limited

Text © Capstone Global Library Limited 2010
First published in hardback in 2010
The moral rights of the proprietor have been asserted.

Edited by Siân Smith, Laura Knowles, Nancy Dickmann, and Rebecca Rissman
Designed by Joanna Hinton-Malivoire
Original Illustrations © Capstone Global Library Ltd. 2010
Illustrated by Tony Wilson
Picture research by Ruth Blair and Mica Brancic
Production by Duncan Gilbert and Victoria Fitzgerald
Originated by Capstone Global Library Ltd
Printed and bound in China by Leo Paper Group

ISBN 978 0 431 19504 9
14 13 12 11 10
10 9 8 7 6 5 4 3 2 1

British Library Cataloguing in Publication Data
Guillain, Charlotte.
Our hearts. -- (Acorn. Our bodies)
1. Heart--Juvenile literature.
I. Title II. Series
612.1'7-dc22

Acknowledgements
We would like to thank the following for permission to reproduce photographs: Corbis pp.**8** (© Stephanie Weiler/zefa), **9** (© Hannah Mentz/zefa), **10** (© John-Francis Bourke/zefa), **17**, **18** (© moodboard), **20** (© Randy Faris); iStockphoto p.**21**; Photolibrary pp.**4**, **22** (© OJO Images), **5** (© Photoalto), **14** (© Tips Italia), **16** (© Photoalto), **23** (© Tips Italia); Science Photo Library pp.**11**, **23** (© Medi-Mation); Shutterstock p.**19** (© Jacek Chabraszewski).

Front cover photograph of children jumping down a sand dune reproduced with permission of Photolibrary (© Swell Media/Uppercut Images). Back cover photograph reproduced with permission of Photolibrary (Photoalto).

Every effort has been made to contact copyright holders of material reproduced in this book. Any omissions will be rectified in subsequent printings if notice is given to the publishers.

Contents

Body parts

Our bodies have many parts.

head

skin

arm

foot

leg

Our bodies have parts on the outside.

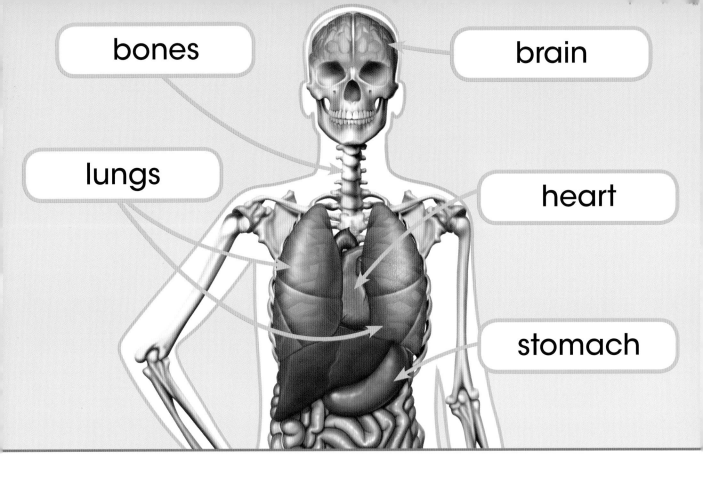

bones

brain

lungs

heart

stomach

Our bodies have parts on the inside.

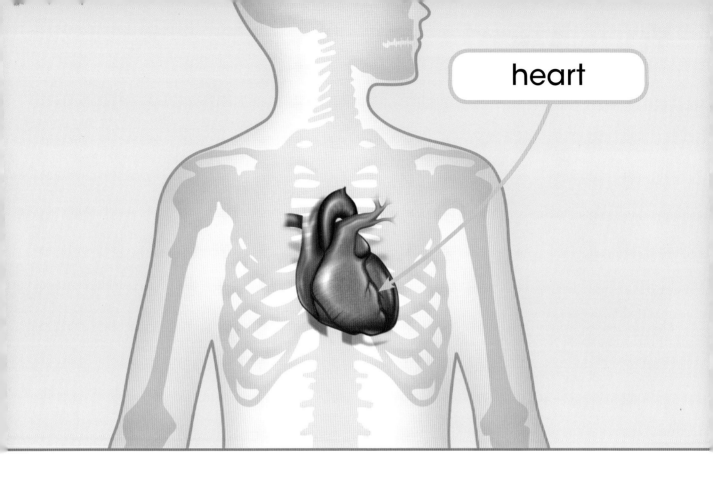

heart

Your heart is inside your body.

Your heart

You cannot see your heart.

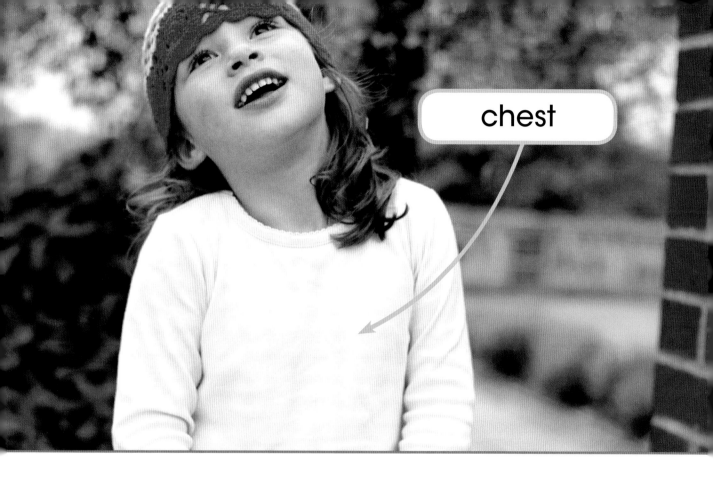

chest

Your heart is inside your chest.

fist

Your heart is about the size of your fist.

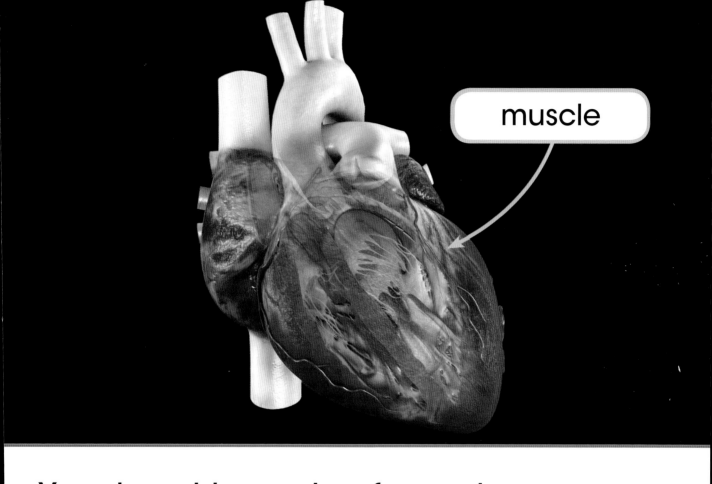

muscle

Your heart is made of muscle.

Muscles can make things move.

Blood

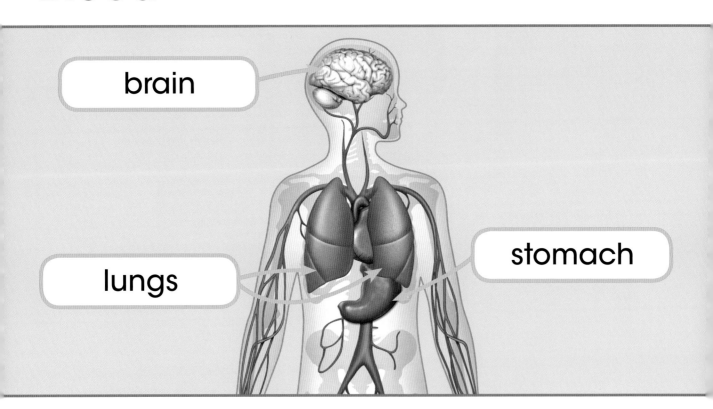

brain

lungs

stomach

Your body parts need blood.

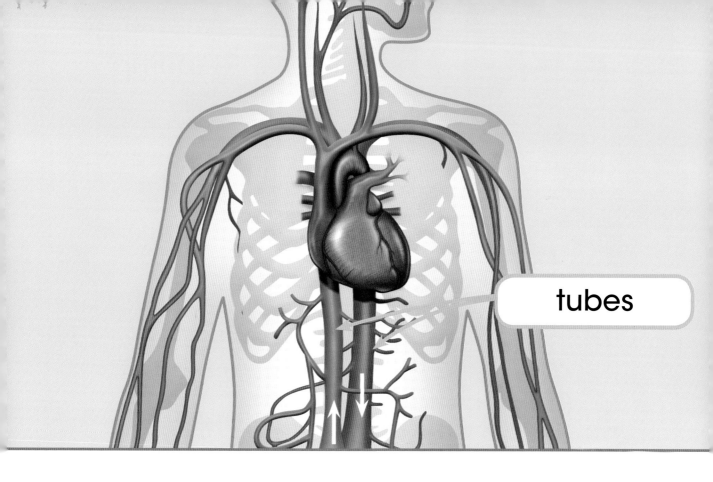

tubes

Blood moves around your body in tubes.

pump

Your heart is like a pump. A pump pushes air into a tyre.

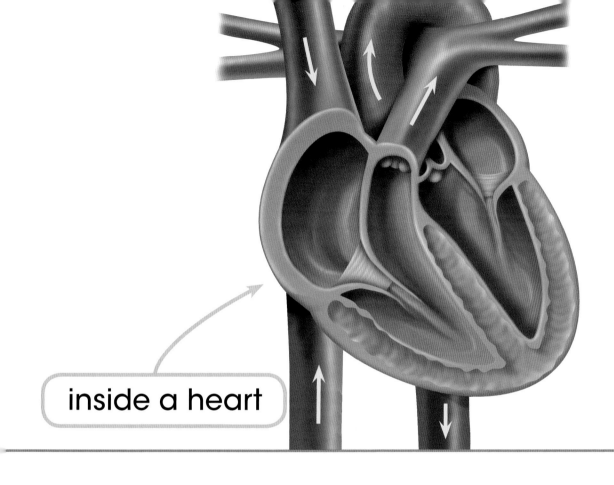

inside a heart

Your heart pushes blood around your body.

Heart beat

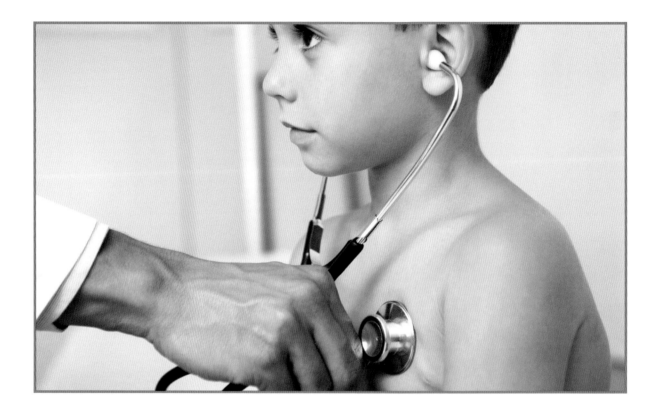

You can hear your heart beat.

You can feel your heart beat.

When you are still, your heart
beats slowly.

When you run, your heart
beats fast.

Staying healthy

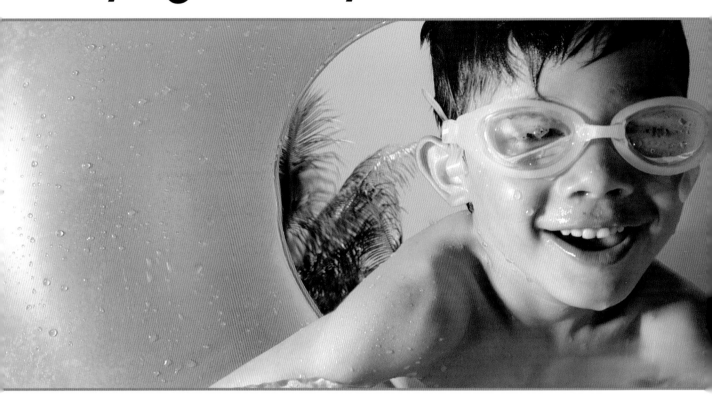

You can exercise to help your heart.

You can eat healthy food to help your heart.

Quiz

Where in your body is your heart?

Answer on page 24

Picture glossary

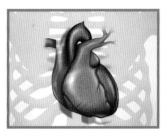

heart part of your body inside your chest. Your heart pushes blood around your body.

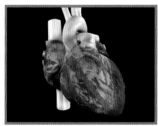

muscle stretchy part inside your body. Muscles can make things move.

pump something you use to push air into a tyre

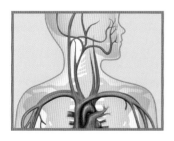

tube a long, thin pipe like a hose. Things can move along inside tubes because they have an empty space in the middle.

Index

Answer to quiz on page 22: Your heart is in your chest.

Notes to parents and teachers

Before reading

Ask the children to name the parts of their body they can see on the outside. Then ask them what parts of their body are inside. Make a list of them together and see if the children know what each body part does, for example, food goes into their stomachs. Discuss where their hearts are and see if anyone knows what our hearts do.

After reading

• Take the children outside and ask them to hold their hands against their chests. Can they feel their heart beat? Then tell them to run around for five minutes. When they stop, ask them to feel their heart beating in their chest again. What do they notice?

• Make a healthy heart poster together. Put a picture of a heart in the middle and ask each child to draw a picture of food or an activity that is good for our hearts. Stick the children's pictures around the heart and put the poster up in the school.